No.	Date	Income	Expenses	Notes	Total
				GW00385261	

No.	Date	Income	Expenses	Notes	Total

No.	Date	Income	Expenses	Notes	Total

No.	Date	Income	Expenses	Notes	Total

No.	Date	Income	Expenses	Notes	Total

No.	Date	Income	Expenses	Notes	Total

No.	Date	Income	Expenses	Notes	Total

No.	Date	Income	Expenses	Notes	Total

No.	Date	Income	Expenses	Notes	Total

No.	Date	Income	Expenses	Notes	Total

No.	Date	Income	Expenses	Notes	Total

No.	Date	Income	Expenses	Notes	Total

No.	Date	Income	Expenses	Notes	Total

No.	Date	Income	Expenses	Notes	Total

No.	Date	Income	Expenses	Notes	Total

No.	Date	Income	Expenses	Notes	Total

No.	Date	Income	Expenses	Notes	Total

No.	Date	Income	Expenses	Notes	Total

No.	Date	Income	Expenses	Notes	Total

No.	Date	Income	Expenses	Notes	Total

No.	Date	Income	Expenses	Notes	Total

No.	Date	Income	Expenses	Notes	Total

No.	Date	Income	Expenses	Notes	Total

No.	Date	Income	Expenses	Notes	Total

No.	Date	Income	Expenses	Notes	Total

No.	Date	Income	Expenses	Notes	Total

No.	Date	Income	Expenses	Notes	Total

No.	Date	Income	Expenses	Notes	Total

No.	Date	Income	Expenses	Notes	Total

No.	Date	Income	Expenses	Notes	Total

No.	Date	Income	Expenses	Notes	Total

No.	Date	Income	Expenses	Notes	Total

No.	Date	Income	Expenses	Notes	Total

No.	Date	Income	Expenses	Notes	Total

No.	Date	Income	Expenses	Notes	Total

No.	Date	Income	Expenses	Notes	Total

No.	Date	Income	Expenses	Notes	Total

No.	Date	Income	Expenses	Notes	Total

No.	Date	Income	Expenses	Notes	Total

No.	Date	Income	Expenses	Notes	Total

No.	Date	Income	Expenses	Notes	Total

No.	Date	Income	Expenses	Notes	Total

No.	Date	Income	Expenses	Notes	Total

No.	Date	Income	Expenses	Notes	Total

No.	Date	Income	Expenses	Notes	Total

No.	Date	Income	Expenses	Notes	Total

No.	Date	Income	Expenses	Notes	Total

No.	Date	Income	Expenses	Notes	Total

No.	Date	Income	Expenses	Notes	Total

No.	Date	Income	Expenses	Notes	Total

No.	Date	Income	Expenses	Notes	Total

No.	Date	Income	Expenses	Notes	Total

No.	Date	Income	Expenses	Notes	Total

No.	Date	Income	Expenses	Notes	Total

No.	Date	Income	Expenses	Notes	Total

No.	Date	Income	Expenses	Notes	Total

No.	Date	Income	Expenses	Notes	Total

No.	Date	Income	Expenses	Notes	Total

o.	Date	Income	Expenses	Notes	Total

No.	Date	Income	Expenses	Notes	Total

No.	Date	Income	Expenses	Notes	Total

No.	Date	Income	Expenses	Notes	Total

No.	Date	Income	Expenses	Notes	Total

No.	Date	Income	Expenses	Notes	Total

o.	Date	Income	Expenses	Notes	Total

No.	Date	Income	Expenses	Notes	Total

No.	Date	Income	Expenses	Notes	Total

No.	Date	Income	Expenses	Notes	Total

No.	Date	Income	Expenses	Notes	Total

No.	Date	Income	Expenses	Notes	Total

o.	Date	Income	Expenses	Notes	Total

No.	Date	Income	Expenses	Notes	Total

No.	Date	Income	Expenses	Notes	Total

No.	Date	Income	Expenses	Notes	Total

No.	Date	Income	Expenses	Notes	Total

No.	Date	Income	Expenses	Notes	Total

o.	Date	Income	Expenses	Notes	Total

No.	Date	Income	Expenses	Notes	Total

No.	Date	Income	Expenses	Notes	Total

No.	Date	Income	Expenses	Notes	Total

No.	Date	Income	Expenses	Notes	Total

No.	Date	Income	Expenses	Notes	Total

No.	Date	Income	Expenses	Notes	Total

No.	Date	Income	Expenses	Notes	Total

No.	Date	Income	Expenses	Notes	Total

No.	Date	Income	Expenses	Notes	Total

No.	Date	Income	Expenses	Notes	Total

No.	Date	Income	Expenses	Notes	Total

o.	Date	Income	Expenses	Notes	Total

No.	Date	Income	Expenses	Notes	Total

No.	Date	Income	Expenses	Notes	Total

No.	Date	Income	Expenses	Notes	Total

No.	Date	Income	Expenses	Notes	Total

No.	Date	Income	Expenses	Notes	Total

o.	Date	Income	Expenses	Notes	Total

No.	Date	Income	Expenses	Notes	Total

No.	Date	Income	Expenses	Notes	Total

No.	Date	Income	Expenses	Notes	Total

No.	Date	Income	Expenses	Notes	Total

No.	Date	Income	Expenses	Notes	Total

Date	Income	Expenses	Notes	Total

No.	Date	Income	Expenses	Notes	Total

No.	Date	Income	Expenses	Notes	Total

No.	Date	Income	Expenses	Notes	Total

No.	Date	Income	Expenses	Notes	Total

No.	Date	Income	Expenses	Notes	Total

o.	Date	Income	Expenses	Notes	Total

No.	Date	Income	Expenses	Notes	Total

Printed in Great Britain
by Amazon